MUSHROOM
COOKBOOK

Consultant Editor:
Valerie Ferguson

LORENZ BOOKS

Contents

Introduction

There are over a thousand varieties of mushroom known to be edible. Which types are best to eat is a matter of personal taste, but it is generally agreed that wild mushrooms have a stronger, more distinctive flavour than cultivated varieties. However, nowadays, many exotic varieties, such as ceps, chanterelles and oyster mushrooms, are also cultivated and their flavour is virtually indistinguishable from those picked wild.

The unique flavour and texture of mushrooms makes them an immensely versatile ingredient. Poultry and game taste good with mushroom flavours. For example, try the delicate richness of chanterelle, saffron milk-cap or St George's mushroom with chicken, or the morel with duck. Beef is the perfect match for the open field, horse and parasol mushroom. Fresh fish and shellfish are also ideal ingredients to accompany a selection of wild mushrooms.

For centuries wild mushrooms have been valued as an alternative to meat and are being rediscovered by vegetarians today for their value, flavour, texture and goodness. This book embraces all the above – a celebration of the versatile mushroom.

Types of Mushroom

Nowadays, many different kinds of mushroom are available from supermarkets. Unless you are knowledgeable about mushrooms, it is dangerous to pick them from the wild.

Button/White Mushrooms

Cultivated mushrooms are widely available. They are sold as button mushrooms when very young and tiny, closed cap when slightly larger, and open capped or open cup when larger still. They have ivory or white caps with pink or beige gills that darken as they mature. All have a pleasant, unassuming flavour. Fry them briskly so that their moisture evaporates.

Chestnut Mushrooms

Also known as champignons de Paris, these have a thicker stem and usually have a pale-brown cap, but there are also creamy-white varieties. They have a more pronounced flavour and a meatier texture than white mushrooms. Cook as white mushrooms.

Field Mushrooms

These are the wild relatives of white mushrooms and have a wonderful aroma. They are sometimes available from farm shops. Flat mushrooms, indistinguishable in appearance from field, have probably been cultivated and are also excellent. Both can be fried in butter, oil and garlic, or stuffed.

Ceps

Known as ceps in France and porcini in Italy, they are also called boletus mushrooms after their botanical name *(Boletus edulis).* These meaty, bun-shaped mushrooms have a fine texture and a superb flavour. Instead of gills, they have a spongy texture beneath the cap and, unless they are very young, it is best to scrape this away as it goes soggy when cooked. They can grow to an enormous size, weighing more than 500 g/1¼ lb each. Fry ceps briskly in oil or brush with oil and grill with a little garlic.

Chanterelles

These frilly, trumpet-shaped mushrooms range in colour from cream to vivid yellow. They have a delicate, slightly fruity flavour and a firm texture. They are difficult to clean as their tiny gills trap grit and earth. Rinse them gently under cold running water and shake dry. Gently fry them in butter then cook briskly to evaporate their liquid.

Morels

Appearing in the spring, rather than the autumn, these are cone-shaped with a crinkled, spongy cap that is hollow inside. They have a very fine and distinctive flavour. They need to be thoroughly washed under cold running water as tiny insects tend to creep into their dark crevices. They require longer cooking than most – up to 1 hour.

Oyster Mushrooms

Ear-shaped, these range in colour from greyish brown to pink and yellow, and caps, gills and stem are the same colour. Their texture is quite soft and their flavour strong and delicious. They are now cultivated and widely available. If they are large, tear rather than cut them into pieces. In very large specimens, the stems can be tough and should be discarded. Delicious quickly fried in butter – do not overcook.

Shiitake Mushrooms

These Japanese tree mushrooms are widely available in most supermarkets. They have a meaty, slightly acid flavour and a slippery texture. Shiitake take 3–5 minutes to be cooked through and cannot be flash fried. Excellent in stir-fries.

Dried Mushrooms

Most wild mushrooms are available dried and have an intense flavour. Dried ceps are usually known as porcini, and dried shiitake are often sold as Chinese dried mushrooms. Soak them in warm water for 20–30 minutes to reconstitute.

Techniques

Buying & Storing

Look for mushrooms, whatever the variety, with unblemished and unbruised caps. Avoid any that have discoloured, as they have probably been on supermarket shelves too long. Use paper bags when buying mushrooms in supermarkets, if available. Plastic bags cause mushrooms to sweat in their own heat, eventually turning slippery and unappetizing. If you have no choice or you buy cellophane-wrapped cartons, transfer loose to the bottom of the refrigerator as soon as possible. Use them as soon as possible after purchase; they will keep for only 1–2 days.

Store dried mushrooms in an airtight container for up to a year.

Preparing

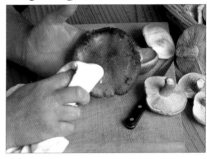

With a few exceptions, such as chanterelles and morels, fresh mushrooms should never be washed but wiped with a damp cloth or kitchen paper. This is partly to avoid increasing their already high water content and also because they should be fried as dry as possible.

Unless the skins are very discoloured, it should not be necessary to peel them, although you will probably need to trim the base of the stems. To stuff large mushrooms, pull off the stalks. The stems of large oyster mushrooms should be discarded and large caps should be torn rather than cut into pieces.

Most wild mushrooms should be cooked to destroy any mild toxins they may contain. White mushrooms, ceps and one or two other varieties may be eaten raw.

To reconstitute dried mushrooms, they need to be soaked in warm water for 20 minutes. Boiling water will make them tough. The water used to soak dried mushrooms should be reserved and added to stocks.

Drying

The process of drying mushrooms intensifies individual flavours and aromas. When fully dried, mushrooms will keep through the winter in air-tight containers.

1 Wipe the mushrooms thoroughly with a damp cloth or kitchen paper and cut away any damaged parts. Slice them thinly. Remove the stems of small chanterelles as they tend to toughen when dried.

2 Lay the sliced mushrooms on a basket tray or a baking sheet lined with several layers of newspaper and a final layer of baking parchment. Put in a warm, well-ventilated place for 2 days. For fast drying, preheat a fan oven to 80°C/180°F/Gas Low, leave the door ajar and dry for 2 hours.

3 When the mushrooms are totally dry, place each variety in an airtight container, label and store in a dark place. If the mushrooms are not fully dry before storing, mould will grow.

Freezing

Firmer varieties, such as white, shiitake, chanterelle and closed field mushrooms are best for freezing.

1 Bring a saucepan of salted water to the boil. Line a tray with baking parchment. Ensure the mushrooms are free from grit and infestation, then trim and slice thickly if large. Simmer in the boiling water for 1 minute.

2 Drain and open freeze on the lined tray for 30-40 minutes. When frozen, turn loosely into plastic bags and keep for up to 6 months in the freezer. Cook from frozen or immerse briefly in boiling water before using.

Wild Mushroom Soup

Beef stock may seem unusual in a vegetable soup, but it helps to strengthen the earthy flavour of the mushrooms.

Serves 4

INGREDIENTS
25 g/1 oz/½ cup dried ceps
250 ml/8 fl oz/1 cup warm water
30 ml/2 tbsp olive oil
15 g/½ oz/1 tbsp butter
2 leeks, thinly sliced
2 shallots, roughly chopped
1 garlic clove, roughly chopped
225 g/8 oz/3¼ cups fresh
    wild mushrooms
about 1.2 litres/2 pints/5 cups beef stock
2.5 ml/½ tsp dried thyme
150 ml/¼ pint/⅔ cup double (heavy) cream
salt and ground black pepper
fresh thyme sprigs, to garnish

1 Put the dried ceps in a bowl, add the water and leave them to soak for 20–30 minutes. Lift out of the liquid and squeeze over the bowl to remove as much of the soaking liquid as possible. Strain all the liquid and reserve. Finely chop the ceps.

2 Heat the oil and butter in a large pan until foaming. Add the leeks, shallots and garlic and cook gently, stirring frequently, for 5 minutes, until softened, but not coloured.

3 Chop or slice the fresh mushrooms and add to the pan. Stir over a medium heat for a few minutes, until they begin to soften. Pour in the stock and bring to the boil. Add the ceps, soaking liquid, thyme and seasoning. Lower the heat, half cover and simmer gently for 30 minutes, stirring occasionally.

4 Pour about three-quarters of the soup into a blender or food processor and process until smooth. Return to the soup left in the pan, stir in the cream and heat through.

5 Check the consistency and add more stock if the soup is too thick. Taste for seasoning. Serve hot, garnished with thyme sprigs.

Shiitake Mushroom & Egg Soup

Osumashi means clear soup and this shiitake and egg *osumashi* goes particularly well with any sushi, as its delicate flavour complements, rather than overpowers.

Serves 4

INGREDIENTS

600 ml/1 pint/2½ cups stock
  made from instant dashi granules
4 shiitake mushrooms, stems removed
  and thinly sliced
5 ml/1 tsp salt
10 ml/2 tsp *usukuchi* soy sauce or light
  soy sauce
5 ml/1 tsp *sake* or dry white wine
2 small eggs
½ punnet cress, to garnish

2 Add the salt, *usukuchi* or light soy sauce and *sake* or dry white wine. Then break the eggs into a small mixing bowl and stir them well with chopsticks.

1 In a large saucepan, bring the stock to the boil, add the shiitake mushrooms and simmer for 1–2 minutes, but do not overcook.

3 Pour the egg into the soup in a thin steady stream, in a circular motion – rather like drawing a spiral shape in the soup. To keep the soup clear, the heat must be high enough to set the egg as soon as it is added.

4 Simmer for a few seconds, until the eggs are cooked. Use a pair of chopsticks to break up the egg in order to serve it equally among 4 bowls.

5 Remove from the heat and transfer to the bowls. Sprinkle with cress and serve immediately.

Tortellini Chanterelle Broth

Savoury-sweet chanterelles combine deliciously with tortellini.

Serves 4

INGREDIENTS
350 g/12 oz fresh spinach and ricotta
    tortellini, or 175 g/6 oz dried
1.2 litres/2 pints/5 cups chicken stock
75 ml/5 tbsp dry sherry
175 g/6 oz/2½ cups fresh chanterelle
    mushrooms, trimmed and sliced, or
    15 g/½ oz/¼ cup dried, soaked
chopped fresh parsley, to garnish

1 Cook the tortellini according to the packet instructions. Drain.

2 Bring the chicken stock to the boil, add the dry sherry and the chanterelle mushrooms and simmer for about 10 minutes.

3 Add the tortellini to the stock. Ladle into four warmed bowls and garnish with the chopped parsley.

COOK'S TIP: For a lighter version, replace the tortellini with 115 g/ 4 oz/2 cups dried vermicelli pasta.

Right: Tortellini Chanterelle Broth (top); Champignons de Paris à la Grecque

Champignons de Paris à la Grecque

Serve with breadsticks for an appetizing and delicious starter.

Serves 4

INGREDIENTS
45 ml/3 tbsp olive oil
15 button (pearl) onions, peeled
½ garlic clove, crushed
675 g/1½ lb/9½ cups chestnut mushrooms,
    halved if large
300 ml/½ pint/1¼ cups boiling chicken stock
75 ml/5 tbsp white wine
10 ml/2 tsp black peppercorns
20 ml/4 tsp coriander seeds
1 sprig thyme
1 small bay leaf
15 ml/1 tbsp wine vinegar
15 cherry tomatoes, skins removed
salt and ground black pepper

1 Heat the oil in a large pan. Add the onions and brown gently over a low heat. Add the garlic and mushrooms, stir and fry gently until the mushrooms soften.

2 Add the stock, wine, peppercorns, coriander seeds, thyme and bay leaf. Cover the surface with greaseproof (waxed) paper. Simmer for 15 minutes. Add the vinegar and season. Add the cherry tomatoes. Allow to cool to room temperature and serve.

Wild Mushroom Salad with Parma Ham

For those not familiar with collecting edible species, larger supermarkets and specialist delicatessens often sell a range of wild mushrooms.

Serves 4

INGREDIENTS
175 g/6 oz Parma ham, thickly sliced
45 ml/3 tbsp butter
450 g/1 lb/6½ cups wild and
    cultivated mushrooms
60 ml/4 tbsp brandy
½ oakleaf lettuce
½ frisée lettuce
15 ml/1 tbsp walnut oil

FOR THE HERB PANCAKES
45 ml/3 tbsp plain (all-purpose) flour
75 ml/5 tbsp milk
1 egg plus 1 egg yolk
60 ml/4 tbsp freshly grated
    Parmesan cheese
45 ml/3 tbsp chopped fresh herbs: parsley,
    thyme, tarragon, marjoram, chives
salt and ground black pepper

1 To make the pancakes, combine the flour with the milk. Beat in the egg and egg yolk, cheese, herbs and seasoning. Place a non-stick frying pan over medium heat and pour in batter to cover the base.

2 When the batter has set, turn the pancake over and cook briefly on the other side. Turn out and cool. Make 3 more pancakes.

3 Roll the pancakes together and cut them into 1 cm/½ in ribbons. Cut the ham into similar-size ribbons and toss together with the pancake ribbons.

4 Heat the butter in a frying pan, add the mushrooms and cook for 6–8 minutes. Add the brandy and ignite. Moisten the salad leaves with walnut oil and distribute among 4 plates. Place the ham and pancake ribbons in the centre, add the mushrooms, season and serve warm.

Mushroom & Almond Pâté

This delightful pâté is the perfect starter to serve vegetarian guests.

Serves 4

INGREDIENTS
30 ml/2 tbsp olive oil or butter
2 onions, chopped
350 g/12 oz/4¾ cups mushrooms, chopped
   or roughly sliced
225 g/8 oz/2 cups ground almonds
½ bunch parsley, stalks removed
salt and ground black pepper
flat leaf parsley, to garnish
thin slices of toast, cucumber, chicory and
   celery sticks, to serve

1 Heat the olive oil or butter in a frying pan over moderate heat. Sauté the onions until golden.

2 Add the mushrooms and continue frying until the juices start to run. Season well with salt and pepper.

3 Put the fried onion and mushrooms into a blender or food processor with the juices. Add the ground almonds and parsley and process briefly. The pâté can either be smooth or you can leave it slightly chunky. Taste again for seasoning.

4 When it has cooled spoon the pâté into individual pots. Garnish with flat leaf parsley and serve with thin slices of toast and sticks of cucumber, chicory and celery.

Stuffed Garlic Mushrooms

This quick and easy starter has a fresh, crispy stuffing.

Serves 4

INGREDIENTS

350 g/12 oz/4¾ cups large open cup
  mushrooms, stems removed
3 garlic cloves, crushed
175 g/6 oz/¾ cup butter, softened
50 g/2 oz/1 cup fresh white breadcrumbs
50 g/2 oz/1 cup chopped fresh parsley
1 egg, beaten
salt and cayenne pepper
8 cherry tomatoes, quartered, to garnish

1 Preheat the oven to 190°C/375°F/
Gas 5. Arrange the mushrooms, cup
side uppermost, on a baking tray. Mix
together the garlic and butter.

2 Divide 115 g/4 oz/½ cup of
the garlic butter between the
mushroom caps.

3 Heat the remaining garlic butter
in a frying pan and lightly fry the
breadcrumbs until golden brown.
Place the chopped parsley in a bowl,
add the breadcrumbs, season to taste
and mix well.

4 Stir in the egg and use the mixture
to fill the mushroom caps. Bake for
10–15 minutes, until the topping has
browned and the mushrooms have
softened. Garnish with quartered
tomatoes and serve.

Buckwheat Blinis with Mushroom Caviar

These little Russian pancakes are traditionally served with fish roe caviar. The term caviar is also given to fine vegetable mixtures called *ikry*.

Serves 4

INGREDIENTS
115 g/4 oz/1 cup strong white bread flour
50 g/2 oz/½ cup buckwheat flour
2.5 ml/½ tsp salt
300 ml/½ pint/1¼ cups milk
5 ml/1 tsp dried yeast
2 eggs, separated
a little vegetable oil
200 ml/7 fl oz/scant 1 cup soured cream or crème fraîche

FOR THE CAVIAR
350 g/12 oz/4¾ cups assorted wild mushrooms
5 ml/1 tsp celery salt
30 ml/2 tbsp walnut oil
15 ml/1 tbsp lemon juice
45 ml/3 tbsp chopped fresh parsley
ground black pepper

1 To make the caviar, trim and chop the mushrooms, then place them in a glass bowl, toss with the celery salt and cover with a weighted plate.

2 Leave the mushrooms for 2 hours. Rinse thoroughly to remove the salt, drain, and press out as much liquid as you can with the back of a spoon. Return them to the bowl and toss with walnut oil, lemon juice, parsley and a twist of pepper. Chill.

3 Sift the flours together with the salt in a large mixing bowl. Warm the milk to about blood temperature. Add the yeast, stirring until dissolved, then pour into the flour. Add the egg yolks and stir to make a smooth batter. Cover with a damp cloth and leave in a warm place.

4 Whisk the egg whites in a clean mixing bowl until they are stiff, then fold them carefully into the pancake batter, which should now have risen.

5 Heat an iron pan or griddle to a moderate temperature. Moisten with oil, then drop spoonfuls of the batter on to the surface. When bubbles rise to the surface, turn them over and cook briefly on the other side. Spoon on the mushroom caviar and top with the soured cream or crème fraîche. Add a twist of pepper and serve.

English Muffins with Sole, Spinach & Mushrooms

Mushrooms have a natural affinity with spinach as in this fish dish. Any flat fish will do, although sole works best.

Serves 2

INGREDIENTS
115 g/4 oz/½ cup butter, plus extra for
    buttering muffins
1 medium onion, chopped
115 g/4 oz/1⅓ cups button (white)
    mushrooms, sliced
2 fresh thyme sprigs, chopped
275 g/10 oz frozen leaf
    spinach, thawed
675 g/1½ lb skinned sole or
    plaice fillet
2 white English muffins, split
60 ml/4 tbsp crème fraîche
salt and ground black pepper

1 Heat 50 g/2 oz/4 tbsp of the butter in a saucepan and add the onion. Cook over a gentle heat until soft, but not coloured.

2 Add the mushrooms and thyme, cover and cook for 2–3 minutes. Remove the lid and increase the heat to drive off excess moisture.

3 Using a spoon, press the spinach in a sieve to extract the moisture.

4 Heat a further 25 g/1 oz/2 tbsp of the butter in a saucepan, add the spinach, heat through and season.

5 Melt the remaining butter in a large frying pan, season the fillets and cook for 4 minutes, turning once.

6 Toast and butter the muffins. Divide the fillets between them, top with spinach and a layer of mushrooms, then finish with a spoonful of crème fraîche and some pepper.

Cod with a Spicy Mushroom Sauce

The fish is grilled before it is added to the sauce to prevent it from breaking up during cooking.

Serves 4

INGREDIENTS
4 cod fillets
15 ml/1 tbsp lemon juice
15 ml/1 tbsp olive oil
1 medium onion, chopped
1 bay leaf
4 black peppercorns, crushed
115 g/4 oz/1⅓ cups button mushrooms
175 ml/6 fl oz/¾ cup
  natural (plain) yogurt
5 ml/1 tsp finely chopped fresh
  root ginger
5 ml/1 tsp finely chopped garlic
2.5 ml/½ tsp garam masala
2.5 ml/½ tsp chilli powder
5 ml/1 tsp salt
15 ml/1 tbsp fresh coriander (cilantro)
  leaves, to garnish
lightly cooked green beans,
  to serve

1 Remove the skin and any bones from the cod fillets. Sprinkle with lemon juice, then cook under a preheated grill (broiler) for about 5 minutes on each side. Remove from the heat and set aside.

2 Heat the oil in a non-stick frying pan and fry the onion with the bay leaf and crushed peppercorns for 2–3 minutes. Lower the heat, then add the mushrooms and stir-fry for a further 4–5 minutes.

3 In a bowl mix together the yogurt, ginger, garlic, garam masala, chilli powder and salt. Pour this over the onions and stir-fry for 3 minutes.

4 Add the cod fillets to the sauce and cook gently for a further 2 minutes. Serve garnished with the coriander and accompanied by lightly cooked green beans.

Fillets of Trout with a Spinach & Field Mushroom Sauce

Delicious served with new potatoes, young carrots and baby corn.

Serves 4

INGREDIENTS
4 brown or rainbow trout, filleted and
skinned to make 8 fillets

FOR THE SPINACH & MUSHROOM SAUCE
75 g/3 oz/6 tbsp unsalted butter
¼ medium onion, chopped
225 g/8 oz/3 cups closed field (portobello)
mushrooms, chopped
300 ml/½ pint/1¼ cups boiling
chicken stock
225 g/8 oz frozen chopped spinach
10 ml/2 tsp cornflour (cornstarch)
15 ml/1 tbsp water
150 ml/¼ pint/⅔ cup crème fraîche
salt and ground black pepper
pinch of grated nutmeg

1 To make the sauce, melt 50 g/
2 oz/¼ cup of the butter in a frying
pan and fry the onion until soft. Add
the mushrooms and cook until the
juices begin to run.

2 Add the stock and the spinach and
continue to cook until the spinach has
completely thawed.

3 Blend the cornflour with the water
and stir into the mushroom mixture.
Simmer gently to thicken.

4 Process the sauce in a food
processor or blender until smooth, add
the crème fraîche and season to taste
with salt and pepper and a pinch of
nutmeg. Turn into a serving jug and
keep warm.

5 Melt the remaining butter in a large
non-stick frying pan. Season the trout
and cook for 6 minutes, turning once.
Serve with the sauce either poured
over or served separately.

VARIATION: Spinach and
mushroom sauce is also good with
fillets of cod, haddock and sole.

Creamy Fish & Mushroom Pie

Fish pie is a healthy and hearty dish for a hungry family. To help the fish go further, mushrooms provide both flavour and nourishment.

Serves 4

INGREDIENTS
225 g/8 oz/3¼ cups assorted wild and
    cultivated mushrooms, trimmed
    and quartered
675 g/1½ lb cod or haddock fillet, skinned
    and diced
600 ml/1 pint/2½ cups boiling milk
salt and ground black pepper

FOR THE TOPPING
900 g/2 lb floury potatoes, peeled
    and quartered
25 g/1 oz/2 tbsp butter
150 ml/¼ pint/⅔ cup milk
pinch of grated nutmeg

FOR THE SAUCE
50 g/2 oz/¼ cup unsalted butter
1 medium onion, chopped
½ celery stick, chopped
50 g/2 oz/½ cup plain (all-purpose) flour
10 ml/2 tsp lemon juice
45 ml/3 tbsp chopped fresh parsley

1 Preheat the oven to 200°C/400°F/
Gas 6. Butter an ovenproof dish, scatter
in the mushrooms and fish, and season.
Pour on the milk, cover and cook in
the oven for 20 minutes. Using a
slotted spoon, transfer the fish and
mushrooms to a 1.5 litres/2½ pints/
6¼ cup ovenproof dish. Reserve the
poaching liquid.

2 Cover the potatoes with cold water,
add a good pinch of salt and boil for
20 minutes. Drain and mash with the
butter and milk. Season well with salt,
pepper and nutmeg.

3 To make the sauce, melt the butter
in a saucepan, add the onion and
celery and fry until soft. Stir in the
flour, then remove from the heat.

4 Slowly add the reserved liquid,
stirring until absorbed. Return to the
heat, stir and simmer to thicken. Add
the lemon juice and parsley, season,
then add to the fish.

5 Top with the mashed potato and return to the oven for 30–40 minutes, until golden brown.

VARIATION: For a stronger flavour, you can substitute half the quantity of fish for smoked cod or haddock. Use undyed smoked fish if you prefer.

Fresh Tuna Shiitake Teriyaki

Teriyaki is a sweet soy marinade usually used to glaze meat. Here teriyaki enhances fresh tuna steaks served with rich shiitake mushrooms.

Serves 4

INGREDIENTS
4 x 175 g/6 oz fresh tuna steaks
150 ml/¼ pint/⅔ cup teriyaki sauce
175 g/6 oz/2½ cups shiitake
    mushrooms, sliced
225 g/8 oz white radish, peeled
2 large carrots, peeled
salt
boiled rice, to serve

2 Preheat a moderate grill (broiler) or barbecue. Remove the tuna steaks from the marinade and reserve the marinade. Cook the tuna steaks for 8 minutes, turning once.

1 Season the tuna steaks with a sprinkling of salt, then set aside for 20 minutes for it to penetrate. In a bowl, pour half the teriyaki sauce over the fish and in a separate bowl pour the remainer of the teriyaki sauce over the shiitake mushrooms and leave both to marinate for a further 20–30 minutes, or longer if possible.

3 Transfer the mushrooms and marinade to a stainless steel saucepan and simmer for 3–4 minutes.

4 Slice the radish and carrot thinly, then shred finely with a chopping knife. Arrange in heaps on 4 serving plates and add the fish, with the mushrooms and sauce poured over. Serve with boiled rice.

COOK'S TIP: Teriyaki sauce is available from Chinese stores and most large supermarkets.

31

Puff Pastry Salmon with a Chanterelle Cream Filling

Salmon and chanterelles work well together in this special occasion dish.

Serves 6

INGREDIENTS
2 x 350 g/12 oz puff pastry, thawed if frozen
1 egg, beaten, to glaze
2 large salmon fillets, about 900 g/2 lb total
    weight, skinned and boned
400 ml/14 fl oz/1⅔ cups dry white wine
1 small carrot
1 small onion, halved
½ celery stick, chopped
1 thyme sprig

FOR THE CHANTERELLE CREAM
25 g/1 oz/2 tbsp unsalted butter
2 shallots, chopped
225 g/8 oz/3¼ cups chanterelles, sliced
75 ml/5 tbsp white wine
150 ml/¼ pint/⅔ cup double (heavy) cream
45 ml/3 tbsp chopped fresh chervil
30 ml/2 tbsp chopped fresh chives

FOR THE HOLLANDAISE SAUCE
175 g/6 oz/¾ cup unsalted butter
2 egg yolks
10 ml/2 tsp lemon juice
salt and ground black pepper

1 Preheat the oven to 200°C/400°F/
Gas 6. Roll out the pastry to form a
rectangle 10 cm/4 in longer and 5
cm/2 in wider than the fillets. Trim
into a fish shape, decorate with a pastry
cutter and glaze with beaten egg.

2 Chill for about 1 hour and then
bake for 30–35 minutes, until well
risen and golden. Remove from the
oven and split open horizontally.
Reduce the oven temperature to
160°C/325°F/Gas 3.

3 For the chanterelle cream, fry the
shallots gently in butter until soft, but
not coloured. Add the mushrooms and
cook until their juices begin to run.
Pour in the wine, increase the heat and
evaporate the juices. Add the cream
and herbs and bring to a simmer.
Season well, transfer to a bowl, cover
and keep warm.

4 Place the salmon in a fish kettle or
roasting tin. Add the wine, carrot,
onion, celery, thyme and enough water
to cover. Bring to the boil over a low
heat. As soon as the water begins to
tremble, remove from the heat, cover
and set aside for 30 minutes.

5 For the sauce, melt the butter, skim the surface and pour into a jug, leaving behind the milky residue. Place the yolks and 15 ml/1 tbsp of water in a bowl over a pan of simmering water. Whisk until thick. Remove from the heat and slowly whisk in the butter. Add the lemon juice and season.

6 Place a salmon fillet on the base of the pastry, spread with the chanterelle cream and cover with the second salmon fillet. Cover with the top of the pastry "fish" and warm through in the oven for about 10–15 minutes. Serve with the hollandaise sauce handed around separately.

Scallops with Mushrooms

This dish has been a classic on Parisian bistro menus since the 1920s – it makes an appealing starter, or serve it as a rich and elegant main course.

Serves 2–4

INGREDIENTS
250 ml/8 fl oz/1 cup dry
    white wine
120 ml/4 fl oz/½ cup water
2 shallots, finely chopped
1 bay leaf
450 g/1 lb shelled scallops, rinsed
40 g/1½ oz/3 tbsp butter
40 g/1½ oz/⅓ cup plain (all-purpose)
    flour
90 ml/6 tbsp whipping cream
pinch of freshly grated nutmeg
175 g/6 oz/2½ cups mushrooms,
    thinly sliced
45–60 ml/3–4 tbsp dry breadcrumbs
salt and ground black pepper

1 Combine the wine, water, shallots and bay leaf in a medium saucepan. Bring to the boil, then reduce the heat to low and simmer for 10 minutes. Add the scallops, cover and simmer for 3–4 minutes, until they are opaque.

2 Remove the scallops from the cooking liquid with a slotted spoon and boil the liquid until reduced to 175 ml/6 fl oz/¾ cup. Strain and reserve the liquid.

3 Remove the tough muscle from the side of the scallops and discard. Slice the scallops in half crossways.

4 Melt 25 g/1 oz/2 tbsp of the butter in a heavy saucepan over a medium heat. Stir in the flour and cook for 2 minutes. Add the reserved liquid, whisking vigorously until smooth, then whisk in the cream and season with salt, freshly ground black pepper and nutmeg. Reduce the heat to low and simmer, stirring frequently, for 10 minutes.

COOK'S TIP: Fresh scallops have the best flavour, but frozen can also be used.

5 Melt the remaining butter in a frying pan over a medium heat. Add the mushrooms and cook, stirring frequently, for about 5 minutes, until lightly browned. Stir the mushrooms into the sauce.

6 Preheat the grill (broiler). Add the scallops to the sauce and adjust the seasoning. Spoon the mixture into 4 individual gratin dishes and sprinkle with breadcrumbs. Grill (broil) until golden brown and bubbly.

Chicken Fricassée Forestier

The term fricassée is used to describe a light stew, usually of chicken that is first sautéed in butter. Serve with rice, young carrots and baby corn.

Serves 4

INGREDIENTS

3 chicken breasts, skinned and sliced
50 g/2 oz/¼ cup unsalted butter
15 ml/1 tbsp vegetable oil
115 g/4 oz unsmoked rindless streaky (fatty) bacon, cut into pieces
75 ml/5 tbsp dry sherry or white wine
1 medium onion, chopped
350 g/12 oz/4¾ cups assorted wild mushrooms, trimmed and sliced
40 g/1½ oz/⅓ cup plain (all-purpose) flour
550 ml/18 fl oz/2½ cups chicken stock
10 ml/2 tsp lemon juice
60 ml/4 tbsp chopped fresh parsley
salt and ground black pepper

2 Return the frying pan to the heat and brown the sediment, stirring constantly. Add the sherry or wine and stir to deglaze. Pour the sherry liquid over the chicken and wipe the pan clean with kitchen paper.

3 Fry the onion in the remaining butter until golden brown. Add the sliced mushrooms and cook, stirring frequently, for 6–8 minutes, until their juices begin to run. Stir in the flour, then remove from the heat. Gradually add the stock and stir until the flour is completely absorbed and the sauce is lump-free.

VARIATION: This dish can also be made using other cuts of uncooked skinned chicken. You could even try using turkey, if preferred.

1 Season the chicken with pepper. Heat half the butter and the oil in a large, heavy frying pan and brown the chicken and bacon. Transfer to a shallow dish and pour off any excess fat.

4 Add the cooked chicken and bacon with the sherry juices, return to a moderate heat and stir to thicken. Simmer for 10–15 minutes to combine the flavours, then add the lemon juice, chopped fresh parsley and seasoning.

Mushroom Picker's Paella

Serves 4

INGREDIENTS

45 ml/3 tbsp olive oil

1 medium onion, chopped

1 small bulb fennel, sliced

225 g/8 oz/3¼ cups assorted wild and
cultivated mushrooms, trimmed and sliced

1 garlic clove, crushed

3 chicken legs, chopped through the bone

350 g/12 oz/1⅔ cups short-grain Spanish
or Italian rice

900 ml/1½ pints/3¾ cups boiling
chicken stock

pinch of saffron strands or 1 sachet of
saffron powder

1 thyme sprig

400 g/14 oz can butter (lima) beans, drained

75 g/3 oz/¾ cup frozen peas

1 Heat the olive oil in a large frying
pan. Add the onion and fennel and fry
gently for 3–4 minutes.

2 Add the mushrooms and garlic
and cook until the juices begin to
run, then increase the heat to
evaporate the juices. Add the chicken
pieces and fry briefly. Add the
remaining ingredients and simmer
for 15 minutes.

3 Remove from the heat and cover
the surface of the paella with a round
of greased greaseproof paper. Cover
the paper with a clean dish towel and
allow the paella to finish cooking in
its own heat for about 5 minutes.
Uncover and serve.

Chicken with Wild Mushrooms

Tender chicken pieces are folded into a rich soured cream sauce.

Serves 4

INGREDIENTS
30 ml/2 tbsp vegetable oil
1 leek, finely chopped
4 chicken breasts, skinned and sliced
225 g/8 oz/3¼ cups wild mushrooms,
   sliced if large
15 ml/1 tbsp brandy
pinch of grated nutmeg
1.5 ml/¼ tsp chopped fresh thyme
150 ml/¼ pint/⅔ cup dry
   white vermouth
150 ml/¼ pint/⅔ cup chicken stock
6 green olives, stoned and quartered
150 ml/¼ pint/⅔ cup soured cream
salt and ground black pepper
thyme and croûtons, to garnish

1 Heat the oil in a large frying pan and cook the leek until softened but not browned. Add the chicken and mushrooms. Fry, stirring occasionally, until just beginning to brown.

2 Pour over the brandy and ignite with care. When the flames have died down, stir in the nutmeg, thyme, vermouth and chicken stock, and season to taste.

3 Bring to the boil, lower the heat and simmer for 5 minutes. Stir in the olives and most of the soured cream. Reheat gently, but do not allow to boil. Garnish with the remaining soured cream, thyme and croûtons.

Duck with Chinese Mushrooms & Ginger

The delicious combination of ingredients in this recipe give it a truly oriental flavour. Make a duck stock to enhance the flavours.

Serves 4

INGREDIENTS
2.5 kg/5½ lb duck
5 ml/1 tsp granulated (white) sugar
50 ml/2 fl oz/¼ cup light soy sauce
2 garlic cloves, crushed
8 dried Chinese mushrooms, soaked
   in 350 ml/12 fl oz/1½ cups warm
   water for 15 minutes
1 onion, sliced
5 cm/2 in piece fresh root ginger, sliced
   and cut in matchsticks
200 g/7 oz baby sweetcorn
½ bunch spring onions (scallions), white
   bulbs left whole, green tops sliced
15–30 ml/1–2 tbsp cornflour (cornstarch),
   mixed to a paste with 60 ml/4 tbsp water
salt and ground black pepper
boiled rice, to serve

1 Cut the duck along the breast, open it up and cut along each side of the backbone. Use the backbone, wings and giblets to make a stock to use later in the recipe. Any trimmings of fat can be rendered in a frying pan, to use later in the recipe.

2 Cut each leg and each breast in half. Place in a bowl, rub with the sugar and then pour over the soy sauce and sprinkle over the crushed garlic.

3 Drain the soaked mushrooms, reserving the soaking liquid. Trim and discard all the stalks, which are too tough to use.

4 Heat the duck fat in a frying pan and cook the onion and ginger, until they give off a good aroma. Push to one side. Lift the duck pieces out of the soy sauce and fry them until browned all over. Add the mushrooms and reserved liquid which has been strained to remove any grit.

5 Add 600 ml/1 pint/2½ cups of the stock or water to the pan. Season, cover and cook over a gentle heat for about 1 hour, until the duck is tender.

VARIATION: Replace the corn with sliced celery and water chestnuts.

6 Add the sweetcorn and the white part of the spring onions and cook for a further 10 minutes. Remove from the heat and add the cornflour paste. Return to the heat and bring to the boil, stirring. Cook for 1 minute, until glossy. Serve, scattered with the spring onion tops, with boiled rice.

Roast Leg of Lamb with a Wild Mushroom Stuffing

When the thigh bone is removed from a leg of lamb a stuffing can be put in its place. This rich stuffing enhances the flavour of the meat.

Serves 4

INGREDIENTS
1.8 kg/4½ lb leg of lamb, boned
watercress, to garnish
roast potatoes and seasonal
  vegetables, to serve

FOR THE WILD MUSHROOM STUFFING
25 g/1 oz/2 tbsp butter
1 shallot or 1 small onion
½ garlic clove, crushed
225 g/8 oz/3¼ cups assorted wild
  and cultivated mushrooms,
  trimmed and chopped
1 thyme sprig, chopped
25 g/1 oz crustless white
  bread, diced
2 egg yolks
salt and ground black pepper

FOR THE WILD MUSHROOM GRAVY
50 ml/2 fl oz/¼ cup red wine
400 ml/14 fl oz/1⅔ cups boiling
  chicken stock
5 g/⅛ oz/2 tbsp dried ceps, bay boletus
  or saffron milk-caps, soaked in warm
  water for 20 minutes
20 ml/4 tsp cornflour (cornstarch)
5 ml/1 tsp Dijon mustard
2.5 ml/½ tsp wine vinegar
knob of butter

1 Preheat the oven to 200°C/400°F/ Gas 6. To make the stuffing, melt the butter in a large, non-stick frying pan and gently fry the shallot or onion without colouring. Add the garlic, mushrooms and thyme and stir until the mushrooms juices begin to run. Increase the heat so that they evaporate.

2 Put the mushrooms into a bowl. Mix in the bread, egg yolks and seasoning, then cool slightly. Season the inside cavity of the lamb and then press the stuffing into the cavity, using a spoon or your fingers. Tie up the end with fine string and then tie around the joint.

3 Place the lamb in a large roasting tin and roast in the preheated oven for 15 minutes per 450 g/1 lb for rare meat and 20 minutes per 450 g/1 lb for medium-rare.

4 Transfer the lamb to a warmed serving plate, cover and keep warm. To make the gravy, spoon off all excess fat from the roasting tin and brown the sediment over a moderate heat. Add the wine and stir to loosen the sediment. Add the stock, the mushrooms and their soaking liquid.

5 Place the cornflour and mustard in a cup and blend with 15 ml/1 tbsp water. Stir into the stock and simmer to thicken. Add the vinegar. Season to taste, stir in the butter and pour into a serving jug. Garnish the lamb with watercress, and serve with the gravy and vegetables.

Pepper Steak with Mushrooms

A luxurious cream and brandy sauce transforms this classic combination.

Serves 4

INGREDIENTS
30 ml/2 tbsp black peppercorns, crushed
2.5 ml/½ tsp hot pepper
    flakes (optional)
4 fillet, sirloin or rump steaks,
    175–225 g/6–8 oz each, well trimmed
45 ml/3 tbsp vegetable oil
15 g/½ oz/1 tbsp butter
150 g/5 oz/2 cups mushrooms, sliced
30 ml/2 tbsp Cognac
150 ml/¼ pint/⅔ cup whipping or
    double (heavy) cream
salt
salad leaves and tomatoes,
    to serve

2 Heat 15 ml/1 tbsp of the oil with the butter in a heavy frying pan that is large enough to accommodate the steaks in one layer. Add the mushrooms and cook over moderate heat, stirring and turning them occasionally, for about 5 minutes.

3 Increase the heat to moderately high and continue cooking until the liquid from the mushrooms has evaporated and they are lightly browned. With a slotted spoon, remove them from the pan and reserve.

1 Combine the peppercorns and hot pepper flakes, if using, and press on to both sides of the steaks.

4 Add the remaining oil to the frying pan. When it is very hot, add the steaks. Fry for 2 minutes on each side or until well browned. Continue cooking until done to your taste. (Test by pressing with your finger.) Remove the steaks from the pan and keep hot.

5 Pour off all the fat from the pan. Add the Cognac and bring to the boil, stirring and scraping the pan juices to deglaze. Add the cream and bring back to the boil. Boil for 1 minute. Stir in the mushrooms and reheat them. Check the seasoning. Put the steaks on warmed serving plates and pour over the cream and brandy sauce. Serve with salad leaves and tomatoes.

Burgundy Steak & Mushroom Pie

Beef cooked in a rich wine sauce is topped with a crisp filo pastry crust.

Serves 4

INGREDIENTS
1 onion, finely chopped
175 ml/6 fl oz/¾ cup beef stock
450 g/1 lb lean chuck steak, cut into
2.5 cm/1 in cubes
120 ml/4 fl oz/½ cup dry
red wine
45 ml/3 tbsp plain (all-purpose) flour
45 ml/3 tbsp water
225 g/8 oz/3 cups button (white) mushrooms,
halved
75 g/3 oz/5 sheets filo pastry
10 ml/2 tsp sunflower oil
salt and ground black pepper
mashed potatoes and runner (green) beans,
to serve

1 Simmer the onion with 120 ml/
4 fl oz/½ cup of the stock in a large,
covered non-stick saucepan for 5
minutes. Uncover and continue to
cook, stirring occasionally, until the
stock has evaporated. Transfer the
onions to a plate and set aside.

2 Add the steak to the saucepan and
dry-fry until the meat is lightly
browned. Return the onions to the
saucepan together with the remaining
stock and the red wine. Cover and
simmer gently for about 1½ hours,
or until tender.

3 Preheat the oven to 190°C/375°F/
Gas 5. Blend the flour with the
water, add to the saucepan and
simmer, stirring constantly until the
sauce has thickened.

4 Add the mushrooms and continue
to cook for 3 minutes. Season to taste
and spoon into a 1.2 litres/2 pints/
5 cup pie dish.

5 Brush a sheet of filo pastry with a
little of the oil, then crumple it up
loosely and place oil-side up over the
filling. Repeat with the remaining
pastry and oil.

6 Bake the pie in the oven for 25–30 minutes, until the pastry is golden brown and crispy. Serve with mashed potatoes and runner beans.

VARIATION: The pie can also be topped with 400 g/14 oz puff pastry. Brush with beaten egg and bake for 25 minutes.

Veal Escalopes with Smoked Cheese & Mushroom Sauce

Sheep's milk cheese melted with cream makes a simple and luxurious sauce for serving with pan-fried veal escalopes smothered with mushrooms. The escalopes are not beaten thin in this recipe.

Serves 4

INGREDIENTS
25 g/1 oz/2 tbsp butter
15 ml/1 tbsp extra virgin olive oil
8 small veal escalopes
2 garlic cloves, crushed
250 g/9 oz/3⅔ cups button (white)
    mushrooms or closed cup mushrooms,
    sliced
115 g/4 oz/1 cup frozen peas, thawed
60 ml/4 tbsp brandy
250 ml/8 fl oz/1 cup whipping cream
150 g/5 oz/1¼ cups smoked sheep's milk
    cheese, diced
salt and ground black pepper
flat leaf parsley, to garnish

1 Melt half the butter with the oil in a large frying pan. Season the escalopes with plenty of pepper and brown them in batches on each side over a high heat. Reduce the heat and cook for about 5 minutes on each side, until just done. The escalopes should feel firm to the touch, but still springy.

VARIATION: This dish would also work well with lean pork steak. However, pork needs to be well cooked and will take longer.

2 Lift the escalopes on to a serving dish and keep hot. Add the remaining butter to the pan. When it melts, stir-fry the garlic and mushrooms for about 3 minutes.

3 Add the peas, pour in the brandy and cook until all the pan juices have been absorbed. Season lightly. Using a slotted spoon, remove the mushrooms and peas and place on top of the veal escalopes.

4 Pour the cream into the pan and stir in the diced cheese. Heat gently until the cheese has melted. Adjust the seasoning and pour over the escalopes and vegetables. Serve immediately, garnished with sprigs of flat leaf parsley.

Mushroom & Fennel Hotpot

Marvellous flavours permeate this unusual vegetarian main course.

Serves 4

INGREDIENTS
25 g/1 oz/½ cup dried shiitake mushrooms
1 small head of fennel or 4 celery sticks
30 ml/2 tbsp olive oil
12 shallots, peeled
225 g/8 oz/3 cups button (white) mushrooms,
    trimmed and halved
300 ml/½ pint/1¼ cups dry cider
25 g/1 oz/½ cup sun-dried tomatoes
30 ml/2 tbsp sun-dried tomato purée (paste)
1 bay leaf
salt and ground black pepper
chopped fresh parsley,
    to garnish

1 Place the dried mushrooms in a bowl. Pour over warm water to cover and set aside for 10 minutes.

2 Slice the fennel or celery sticks and heat the oil in a flameproof casserole. Add the shallots and fennel or celery and sauté over a moderate heat for about 10 minutes, until the mixture is softened and lightly browned.

3 Add the button mushrooms to the fennel or celery then drain the dried mushrooms, reserving the liquid. Add to the pan, cutting up any large pieces.

4 Pour in the cider and stir in the sun-dried tomatoes and the paste. Add the bay leaf. Bring to the boil, then lower the heat, cover and simmer for about 30 minutes. Season to taste.

5 If the mixture seems dry, stir in the reserved liquid from the soaked mushrooms. Reheat briefly, then remove the bay leaf and serve, sprinkled with chopped fresh parsley.

VARIATION: 175 g/6 oz cooked or canned chesnuts could be added 10 minutes before the end of the cooking time, which would give an excellent flavour to the casserole.

Tagliatelle with Mushrooms

For the best flavour, use a mixture of wild and cultivated mushrooms, such as field, chestnut, oyster and chanterelles.

Serves 4

INGREDIENTS
1 small onion, finely chopped
2 garlic cloves, crushed
150 ml/¼ pint/⅔ cup vegetable stock
225 g/8 oz/3¼ cups mixed mushrooms
60 ml/4 tbsp white or red wine
10 ml/2 tsp tomato purée (paste)
15 ml/1 tbsp soy sauce
5 ml/1 tsp chopped fresh thyme
30 ml/2 tbsp chopped fresh parsley
225 g/8 oz fresh sun-dried tomato
    and herb tagliatelle
salt and ground black pepper
shavings of Parmesan cheese,
    to serve (optional)

2 Add the mushrooms (quartered or sliced if large or left whole if small), wine, tomato purée and soy sauce. Cover and cook for 5 minutes.

3 Remove the lid from the pan and boil until the liquid has reduced by half. Stir in the herbs and seasoning.

1 Put the chopped onion and garlic into a medium-size saucepan with the vegetable stock. Cover and cook over a moderate heat for 5 minutes, or until tender.

4 Cook the pasta in a large pan of boiling, salted water until tender, but still firm to the bite. Drain thoroughly and toss lightly with the mushrooms. Serve at once with Parmesan, if using.

Wild Mushroom Pizzettes

Fresh wild mushrooms add a distinctive flavour to the topping of these little pizzas, but a mixture of cultivated mushrooms would do just as well.

Serves 4

INGREDIENTS
45 ml/3 tbsp olive oil
350 g/12 oz/4¾ cups fresh wild mushrooms, washed and sliced
2 shallots, chopped
2 garlic cloves, finely chopped
30 ml/2 tbsp chopped fresh mixed thyme and flat leaf parsley
40 g/1½ oz/½ cup Gruyère cheese, grated
30 ml/2 tbsp freshly grated Parmesan cheese
salt and ground black pepper

FOR THE DOUGH
225 g/8 oz/2 cups strong white flour
2.5 ml/½ tsp salt
5 ml/1 tsp easy-blend (rapid rise) dried yeast
150 ml/¼ pint/⅔ cup warm water
30 ml/2 tbsp olive oil

1 To make the dough, put the flour, salt and easy-blend dried yeast in a food processor and process for a few seconds. Mix together the warm water and olive oil and, with the machine running, gradually add the liquid until the mixture forms a soft dough.

2 Turn out the dough on to a lightly floured surface and knead until smooth and elastic. Place in an oiled bowl, cover with clear film (plastic wrap) and set aside in a warm place for 1 hour, until doubled in size.

3 Preheat the oven to 220°C/425°F/ Gas 7. Heat 30 ml/2 tbsp of the oil in a large frying pan. Add the mushrooms, shallots and garlic and fry over a moderate heat until all the mushroom juices have evaporated. Stir in half the herbs. Season, then set aside to cool.

4 Divide the dough into four pieces and roll out each one on a lightly floured surface to a 13 cm/5 in round. Place well apart on two greased baking sheets, then push up the dough edges to form a thin rim. Brush the pizza bases with the remaining oil and top with the wild mushroom mixture.

5 Mix together the grated Gruyère and Parmesan cheeses, then sprinkle them over the mushroom mixture. Bake for 15–20 minutes, until crisp and golden. Remove the pizzettes from the oven and scatter over the remaining herbs. Serve immediately.

Mushroom Curry

This is a delicious, spicy way of cooking button mushrooms that
goes well with plain boiled rice.

Serves 4

INGREDIENTS
30 ml/2 tbsp oil
2.5 ml/½ tsp cumin seeds
1.5 ml/¼ tsp black peppercorns
4 green cardamom pods
1.5 ml/¼ tsp ground turmeric
1 onion, finely chopped
5 ml/1 tsp ground cumin
5 ml/1 tsp ground coriander
2.5 ml/½ tsp garam masala
1 green chilli, finely chopped
2 garlic cloves, crushed
2.5 cm/1 in piece of root ginger, grated
400 g/14 oz can chopped tomatoes
450 g/1 lb/6 cups button (white) mushrooms,
   halved
chopped fresh coriander (cilantro), to garnish

2 Add the onion and fry for about
5 minutes, until golden. Stir in the
ground cumin, coriander and garam
masala and fry for a further 2 minutes.

3 Add the chilli, garlic and ginger
and fry for 2–3 minutes, stirring
constantly to prevent the spices from
sticking to the pan. Add the tomatoes.
Bring to the boil and simmer for
about 5 minutes.

1 Heat the oil in a large saucepan
over moderate heat and fry the cumin
seeds, peppercorns, cardamom pods
and ground turmeric for 2–3 minutes,
stirring constantly.

4 Add the mushrooms. Cover and simmer over a low heat for about 10 minutes. Garnish with coriander.

COOK'S TIP: Remove the fiery seeds from the fresh green chilli before chopping the flesh. Wear gloves and take care never to rub your eyes after preparing chillies.

Chinese Mushrooms with Cellophane Noodles

Red fermented beancurd adds extra flavour to this hearty vegetarian dish. Look out for it in cans or earthenware pots at Chinese food markets.

Serves 4

INGREDIENTS

115 g/4 oz/2 cups dried Chinese mushrooms
25 g/1 oz/½ cup dried cloud ear (wood ear) mushrooms
115 g/4 oz dried beancurd
30 ml/2 tbsp vegetable oil
2 garlic cloves, finely chopped
2 slices fresh root ginger,
    finely chopped
10 Sichuan or black peppercorns, crushed
15 ml/1 tbsp red fermented beancurd
½ star anise
pinch of sugar
15–30 ml/1–2 tbsp soy sauce
50 g/2 oz cellophane noodles, soaked in
    hot water until soft
salt

1 Soak the Chinese mushrooms and cloud ears separately in bowls of hot water for 30 minutes. Break the dried beancurd into small pieces and soak in water according to the instructions on the packet.

2 Strain the soaked mushrooms, reserving the liquid. Squeeze as much liquid from the mushrooms as possible, then remove and discard the mushroom stems. Cut the cups in half if they are large.

3 The cloud ears should swell to five times their original size. Drain them, rinse thoroughly and drain again. Cut off any gritty parts, then cut each wood ear into two or three pieces.

4 Heat the oil in a heavy-based pan. Add the garlic, ginger and Sichuan or black peppercorns. Fry for a few seconds, then add the mushrooms and red fermented beancurd. Mix lightly and fry for 5 minutes.

5 Add the reserved mushroom liquid to the pan, with sufficient water to completely cover the mushrooms. Add the star anise, sugar and soy sauce, then cover and simmer for 30 minutes.

6 Add the cloud ears and the reconstituted beancurd pieces to the mushroom mixture. Cover and cook for about 10 minutes.

7 Drain the cellophane noodles, add them to the mixture and cook for a further 3 minutes until tender, adding more liquid if necessary. Add salt to taste and serve.

COOK'S TIP: Cloud ears are used extensively in Chinese cooking and can be obtained from Oriental stores.

Mushroom Flan

A sophisticated mushroom flan with a cheese soufflé topping. Serve hot with cranberry relish and Brussels sprouts for a Christmas treat.

Serves 8

INGREDIENTS
225 g/8 oz/2 cups plain (all-purpose) flour
175 g/6 oz/¾ cup butter
10 ml/2 tsp paprika
115 g/4 oz/1⅓ cups grated Parmesan cheese
1 egg, beaten with 15 ml/1 tbsp cold water
15 ml/1 tbsp Dijon mustard

FOR THE FILLING
25 g/1 oz/2 tbsp butter
1 onion, finely chopped
350 g/12 oz/4¾ cups mushrooms, chopped
1–2 garlic cloves, crushed
10 ml/2 tsp dried mixed herbs
15 ml/1 tbsp chopped fresh parsley
50 g/2 oz/1 cup fresh white breadcrumbs
salt and ground black pepper

FOR THE CHEESE TOPPING
25 g/1 oz/2 tbsp butter
25 g/1 oz/¼ cup plain (all-purpose) flour
300 ml/½ pint/1¼ cups milk
25 g/1 oz/⅓ cup grated Parmesan cheese
75 g/3 oz/¾ cup grated Cheddar cheese
1.5 ml/¼ tsp English mustard powder
1 egg, separated

1 For the pastry, rub together the flour and butter to form fine crumbs. Stir in the paprika and Parmesan. Bind to a dough with the egg and water. Knead until smooth, wrap in clear film (plastic wrap) and chill for 30 minutes.

2 For the filling, melt the butter and soften the onion. Add the mushrooms and garlic and cook, stirring, for 5 minutes. Increase the heat and drive off any liquid in the pan. Remove the pan from the heat and stir in the dried herbs, parsley, breadcrumbs and seasoning. Allow to cool.

3 Preheat the oven to 190°C/375°F/ Gas 5. Put a baking tray in the oven. Roll out the pastry and line a 23 cm/ 9 in loose-based flan tin, pressing the pastry well into the edges and making a narrow rim around the top edge. Chill for 20 minutes.

4 For the topping, melt the butter in a pan, stir in the flour and cook for 2 minutes. Blend in the milk. Bring to the boil then simmer for 2–3 minutes. Remove the pan from the heat and stir in the cheeses, mustard powder and egg yolk, and season well. Beat until smooth. Whisk the egg white until it holds soft peaks, then fold into the topping.

5 To assemble the flan, spread the Dijon mustard evenly over the base of the flan case. Spoon in the mushroom filling and level the surface, then pour over the cheese topping. Place the flan on the hot baking tray and bake for 35–45 minutes, until the topping is set and golden brown. Remove the flan from the tin and serve hot.

Mushroom Gougère

A savoury choux pastry ring makes a marvellous main course dish that can be made ahead then baked when required.

Serves 4

INGREDIENTS
115 g/4 oz/1 cup strong plain (all-purpose) flour
2.5 ml/½ tsp salt
75 g/3 oz/6 tbsp butter
200 ml/7 fl oz/scant 1 cup cold water
3 eggs, beaten
75 g/3 oz/¾ cup diced Gruyère cheese

FOR THE FILLING
1 small onion, sliced
1 carrot, coarsely grated
225 g/8 oz/3¼ cups button (white) mushrooms, sliced
40 g/1½ oz/3 tbsp butter or margarine
5 ml/1 tsp tikka or mild curry paste
25 g/1 oz/¼ cup plain (all-purpose) flour
300 ml/½ pint/1¼ cups milk
30 ml/2 tbsp fresh parsley, chopped
salt and ground black pepper
30 ml/2 tbsp flaked almonds, to garnish

1 Preheat the oven to 200°C/400°F/Gas 6. Grease a shallow ovenproof dish about 23 cm/9 in round.

2 To make the choux pastry, first sift the flour and salt on to a sheet of greaseproof paper. In a large saucepan, heat the butter and water until the butter just melts. Do not let the water boil. Fold the paper and shoot the flour into the pan all at once.

3 Off the heat beat the mixture rapidly with a wooden spoon, until it is smooth and comes away from the sides of the pan. Cool for 10 minutes.

4 Beat the eggs gradually into the mixture until it has a soft, but still quite stiff, dropping consistency. You may not need all the egg. Stir in the cheese, then spoon the mixture around the sides of the prepared dish.

5 To make the filling, sauté the onion, carrot and mushrooms in the butter or margarine for 5 minutes. Stir in the curry paste then the flour. Gradually stir in the milk and heat until thickened. Mix in the parsley, season well, then pour into the centre of the choux pastry.

6 Bake for 35–40 minutes, until risen and golden brown, sprinkling on the almonds for the last 5 minutes or so, to toast them, which increases their flavour. Serve at once.

Index

This edition is published by Lorenz Books,
an imprint of Anness Publishing Ltd,
108 Great Russell Street, London WC1B 3NA info@anness.com

www.lorenzbooks.com; www.annesspublishing.com

© Anness Publishing Limited 2014

If you like the images in this book and would like to investigate
using them for publishing, promotions or advertising, please visit
our website www.practicalpictures.com for more information.

Publisher: Joanna Lorenz
Editor: Valerie Ferguson & Helen Sudell
Series Designer: Bobbie Colgate Stone
Designer: Andrew Heath

Recipes contributed by: Catherine Atkinson,
Angela Boggiano, Kit Chan, Carole Clements,
Roz Denny, Shirley Gill, Shehzad Husain,
Christine Ingram, Judy Jackson, Manisha Kanani,
Masaki Koi, Norma Macmillan, Sue Maggs,
Norma Miller, Sallie Morris, Maggie Pannell,
Steven Wheeler, Elizabeth Wolf-Cohen, Jeni Wright

Photography: William Adams-Lingwood, Karl Adamson, Edward
Allwright, James Duncan, John Heseltine, Amanda Heywood,
Ferguson Hill, Janine Hosegood, David Jordan, Patrick
McLeavey, Michael Michaels, Thomas Odulate, Peter Reilly

A CIP catalogue record for this book is available from the
British Library

COOK'S NOTES

Bracketed terms are intended for American readers.

For all recipes, quantities are given in both metric and imperial
measures and, where appropriate, in standard cups and spoons.
Follow one set of measures, but not a mixture, because they are
not interchangeable.

Standard spoon and cup measures are level. 1 tsp = 5ml, 1 tbsp =
15ml, 1 cup = 250ml/8fl oz. Australian standard tablespoons are
20ml. Australian readers should use 3 tsp
in place of 1 tbsp for measuring small quantities.

American pints are 16fl oz/2 cups. American readers should use
20fl oz/2.5 cups in place of 1 pint when measuring liquids.

Electric oven temperatures in this book are for conventional
ovens. When using a fan oven, the temperature will probably
need to be reduced by about 10–20°C/20–40°F. Since ovens
vary, you should check with your manufacturer's instruction
book for guidance.

Medium (US large) eggs are used unless otherwise stated.

PUBLISHER'S NOTE:
Although the advice and information in this book are believed
to be accurate and true at the time of going to press, neither the
authors nor the publisher can accept any legal responsibility or
liability for any errors or omissions that may have been made nor
for any inaccuracies nor for any loss, harm or injury that comes
about from following instructions or advice in this book.